FOLENS FLYING START
Starting Key Stage 2 Science

CONTENTS

2	Animal round up	16	Reading a thermometer
3	Air, land and water	17	Weather wise
4	Food chains	18	Blowing in the wind
5	Ways to move	19	Skates
6	Smudge bugs	20	Drop it!
7	Sight tests	21	In a spin
8	Finger press ups	22	Pretty Polly
9	Jump!	23	Balancing parrot
10	Our changing world	24	It's pneumatic!
11	How do they compare?	25	Shadows
12	House on fire	26	High or low?
13	Dissolving	27	What a noise!
14	It's not fair!	28	Is it attracted?
15	A fair test		

Folens books are protected by international copyright laws. All rights are reserved. The copyright of all materials in this book, except where otherwise stated, remains the property of the publisher and authors. No part of this publication may be reproduced, stored in a retrieval system, or transmitted, in any form or by any means, for whatever purpose, without the written permission of Folens Limited.
© 1994 Folens Limited, on behalf of the authors.
First published 1994 by Folens Limited, Dunstable and Dublin.
ISBN 1 85276717-0
Folens Limited, Apex Business Centre, Boscombe Road, Dunstable, LU5 4RL, England.

© Folens.

Animal round up

- Look closely at the animals in the picture.
  There are 5 pairs of animals that look alike.
- Round up the animals by putting the names of the pairs in the chart.

goldfish

frog

eel

blue-tit

cat

mouse

lizard

seagull

snake

newt

What can you see?	Which animals look like that?	Animal group name
scaly dry skin		
scaly wet skin		
smooth skin		
feathery skin		
hairy skin		

There are 5 special names given to these groups of animals by scientists.
The names are birds, reptiles, amphibians, mammals and fishes.

- Write the names in their correct places on the chart.

How well did I do?

2

© Folens.

Air, land and water

- Sort the animals:

land   water

Key
1 Canada goose
2 mute swan
3 mallard duck
4 kingfisher
5 heron
6 coot
7 great crested grebe
8 tadpole
9 pike
10 salmon

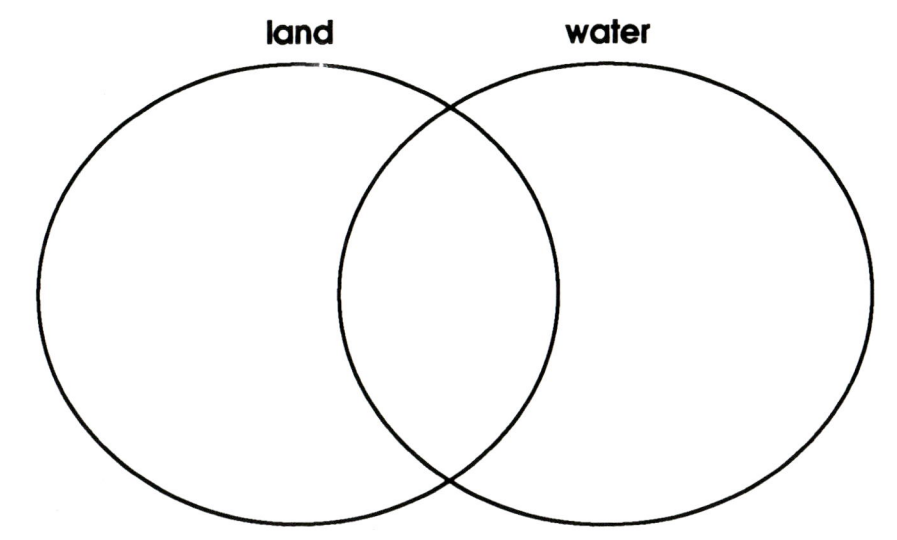

- Think of another way to sort them. (Clue: air.)

How well did I do?

© Folens.

Food chains

A food chain shows that one living thing is eaten by another. Food chains always start with plants and go towards animals.

For example: lettuce leaf ⟶ snail ⟶ thrush

- Make 3 food chains from these living things.

barn owl
harvest mouse
person
cat
grass
goldfish
wheat
sheep
pondweed

- Food chain 1. _____

- Food chain 2. _____

- Food chain 3. _____

How well did I do?

4

© Folens.

Ways to move

- Link the words to the animals.
- Remember: animals may move in more than one way.

fly   crawl   swim

run   hop   creep   walk

- Sort the animals:

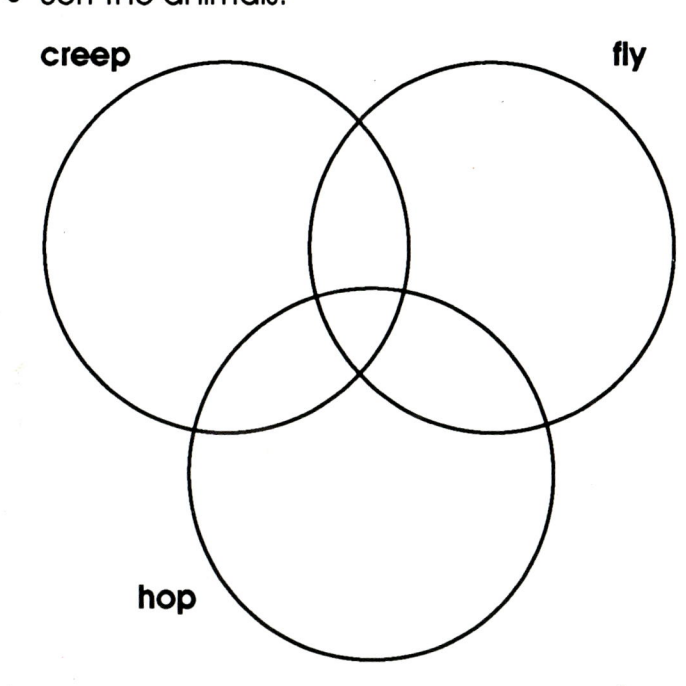

creep   **fly**

hop

Key
1 rabbit
2 adder
3 swallow
4 grey squirrel
5 mole
6 earthworm
7 grasshopper
8 garden spider
9 common lizard
10 caterpillar
11 wagtail
12 common frog
13 tiger moth
14 painted lady
15 garden snail

- Think of another way to sort them.

How well did I do?

© Folens.

Smudge bugs

You need a ruler to measure millimetres.

These are Zena's 25 pet smudge bugs.
You are going to find out how different their sizes are.

- Measure how many millimetres long each bug is.
- Record each measurement by colouring the graph.

1. How many bugs are the biggest size? _____
2. How many bugs are the smallest size? _____
3. What is the most common size of bug? _____

- Invent a new kind of bug.
  Draw it here:

Number of smudge bugs of each length

Length in millimetres

How well did I do?

6

© Folens.

Sight tests

You need:

newspaper

tape measure or ruler

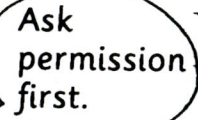

sticky tape.

Ask permission first.

Test your family or friends.
- Tape a page from a newspaper to a door or to a wall.

- Ask someone to point at the smallest printing.
- Move closer, until you can just read the words out loud and get them right!
- Stand still!
  Someone then measures from the tip of your nose to the paper.
- Write this distance on the chart. Test each other and fill in the rest of the chart.

	Distance from the newspaper		
Our names	Both eyes open	Left eye open	Right eye open

If anyone wears glasses, do the test with and then without them on.

Things to talk about afterwards.

1. Do both eyes see equally well? _____
2. How much difference does wearing glasses make? _____
   _____

How well did I do?

7

© Folens.

Finger press ups

You need: watch with 'stopwatch'    clothes peg.

- Test your family and friends.

How many times can you squeeze a clothes-peg in half a minute?

One person will have to time half a minute.

This is how you do a finger press-up

Record

First try

Names	Score with the left hand	Score with the right hand
1		
2		
3		
4		

Second try

Names	Score with the left hand	Score with the right hand
1		
2		
3		
4		

Third try

Names	Score with the left hand	Score with the right hand
1		
2		
3		
4		

Questions

1. Who is the finger press-up champion? _____
2. What was the highest score with the left hand? _____
3. Who had the highest score with the right hand? _____
4. What was the highest total score for the 3 tries? _____
5. Why is it a good idea to do the test 3 times? _____

_____

How well did I do?

© Folens.

Jump!

Do this outdoors.

You need: chalk, tape measure.

You can jump in all directions.
Find out which way you can jump furthest.
- Mark each jump with chalk.
- Measure the jumps.

**Keep away from obstacles!
Take care!**

jump to the right

jump forwards

jump up

1. stretch
2. mark
3. jump with chalky fingers
4. measure to the chalk

jump to the left

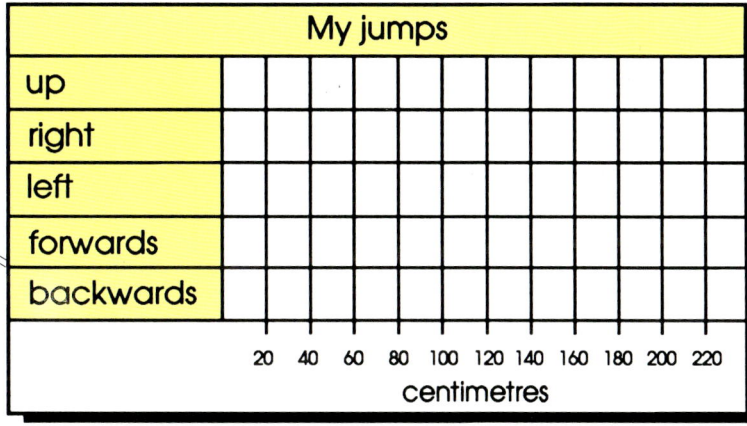

jump backwards

My jumps											
up											
right											
left											
forwards											
backwards											

20 40 60 80 100 120 140 160 180 200 220
centimetres

- Record your jumps on this chart.

- Which was your longest jump? _____

- Which is the easiest way to jump? _____

How well did I do?

© Folens.

Our changing world

The word 'environment' means 'the conditions around us'.

There are lots of things happening to our environment in this picture.
Many of them are spoiling our world.

- Write in this space the things in the picture that are spoiling the environment.

- Write in this space 3 ways that we could improve our environment.

How well did I do?

© Folens.

How do they compare?

You need samples of the materials listed.

Look closely at each material. Feel them.

Think hard about what they are like.

Use the chart to say how the materials are similar to each other, and how they are different.

Materials	How are they alike?	How are they different?
rubber paper		
paper aluminium (kitchen foil)		
aluminium ice		
ice water		
water air		

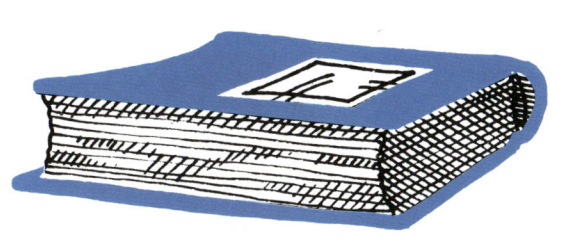

How well did I do?

House on fire

Here is a house with problems!

- Number the fire hazards you can find.
- List the hazards here:

_____   _____

_____   _____

_____   _____

_____   _____

How well did I do?

Dissolving

You need: jar, soil, water, salt, sand, sugar, spoon

Investigate.

- Put a spoonful of soil into a jam jar.
- Add some water and stir it.
- Watch carefully.
- Do the same with all the other materials and record your results below.

Record.

Some materials dissolved in the water.
You could no longer see any small pieces.
We say they are **soluble**.
The materials that did not dissolve are **insoluble**.

Put a tick in the correct box for each material.

material	soluble	insoluble
soil		
sand		
sugar		
salt		

Do not put these materials back into kitchen storage.

- Talk about whether soluble materials dissolve more easily in hot or cold water.

- How do you know? _____

_____

- How can you test your idea? _____

_____

How well did I do?

© Folens.

It's not fair!

Jagtar said: "Washing-up liquid makes water drops spread out."

He made a waxy patch on a scrap of paper by scribbling with a crayon.
Then he used a straw to put a small drop of clean water on the waxy patch.

Jagtar looked carefully at the drop for about a minute.
He dipped the point of the pin in the washing-up liquid and touched the water-drop with the pin point.

Jagtar noticed that the drop spread out over the waxy patch.

Wow! I'm right!

Why is Jagtar's test not a fair one?
(What else could have made the water spread out?)

How would you make the test fair?

How well did I do?

Now turn to page 15.

A fair test

You need: washing up liquid, wax crayons, pin, plastic straw.

- Now do Jagtar's test in a fair way.
  Change one thing at a time.
  Keep everything else the same.

- Record what happens.

  This chart may help.

What I did:		What happened. Water spread out?
Put a drop of water on:	Touched the drop with a pin dipped in washing up liquid? yes ✔ no ✘	yes ✔ no ✘
plain paper	✔	
plain paper	✘	
waxed paper	✔	
waxed paper	✘	

- Was Jagtar right? _____

- How was your test fairer than Jagtar's? _____

_____

_____

_____

How well did I do?

© Folens.

15

Reading a thermometer

There are 2 temperature scales used in weather forecasts. The older scale was devised by Gabriel Fahrenheit and is named after him. The scale which has replaced Fahrenheit is called Celsius or Centigrade.

Celsius

Each small line is one degree Celsius (1°C)

Every 10°C is labelled

Boiling point of water is 100°C

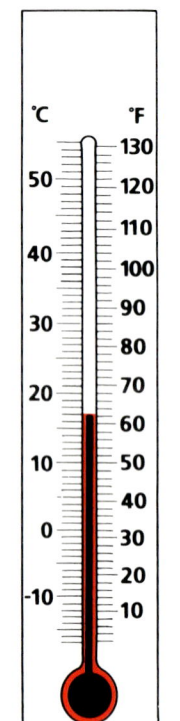

Fahrenheit

Each small line is 2 degrees Fahrenheit (2°F)

Every 10°F is labelled

Boiling point of water is 212°F

WORK TO DO

- This temperature is ___ °C
- Freezing point of water is ___ °C

- This temperature is ___ °F
- Freezing point of water is ___ °F

What is the temperature?

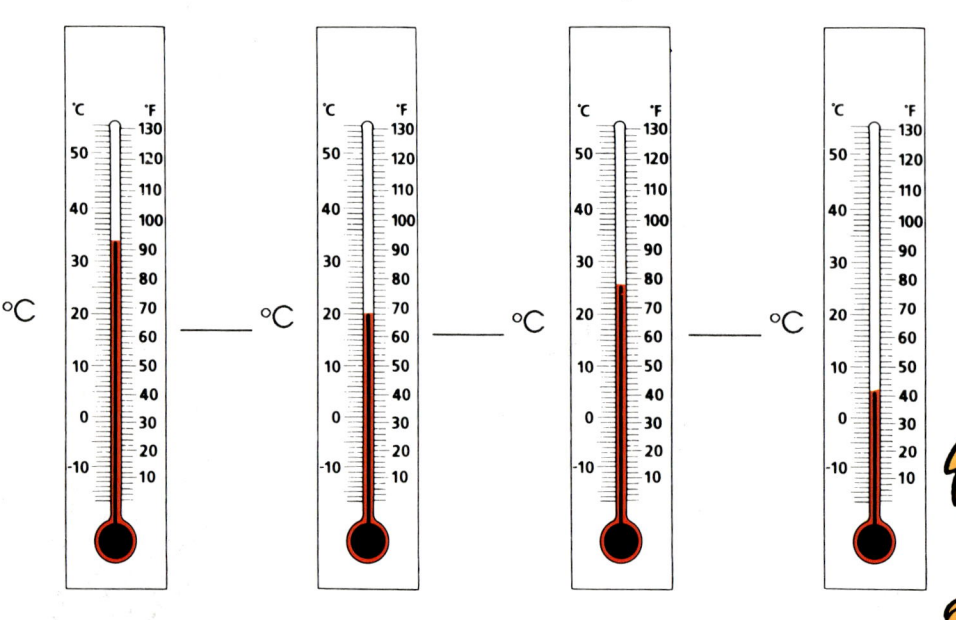

___ °C   ___ °C   ___ °C   ___ °C

How well did I do?

- What is your room's temperature today? _____ °C

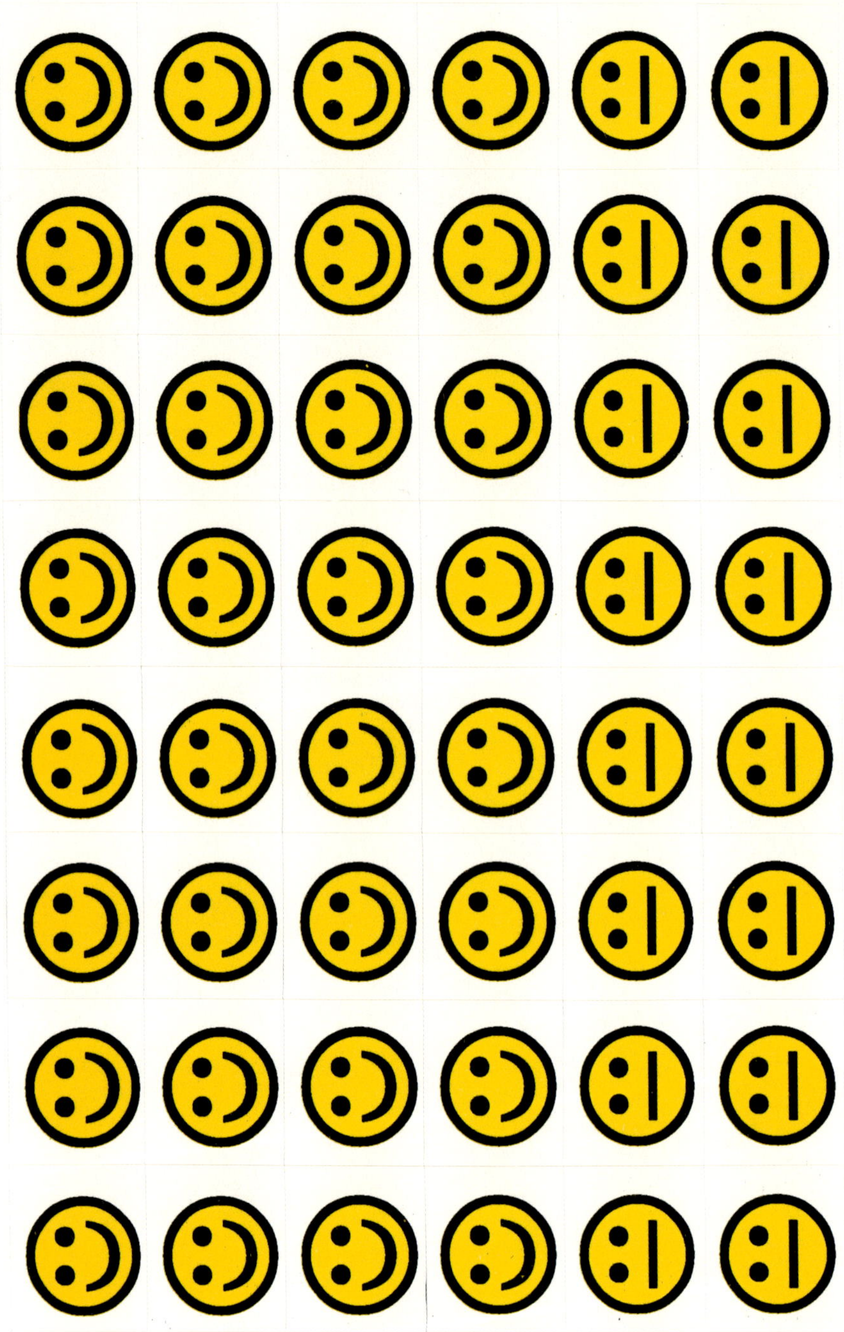

Weather wise

You have probably seen a television weather map of the whole country or the part where you live.
The weather forecasters use small pictures called symbols to show what the weather will be like.

Yellow circles with numbers inside them show the temperature in degrees Celsius. Blue circles with numbers inside show the number of degrees Celsius below freezing. Of course, you can guess what the weather symbol F O G means.

- Write the number of the symbol next to its correct meaning on the chart.

	Weather symbol meanings
	Rain
	Bright sunshine: temperature 25°C
	Snow
	Thunderstorm
	Rain with sunny intervals
	Sleet
	Thick dull cloud
	Fine but cloudy
	Cloudy with sunny intervals

Make a weather map for a treasure island.

How well did I do?

© Folens.

Blowing in the wind

Where is the wind coming from?

- Look at the points of the compass.

- Now look at the sign below.

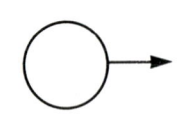

The sign shows where the wind comes from. The arrow shows where the wind is going. This wind has come from the west, and is going east. It is a **westerly wind**.

- Look at the signs below.
- With a helper work out what sort of winds they are and complete the table. Use the compass above to help you and remember to put where the wind is coming from.

Symbol	Type of wind
a	southerly wind
b	
c	
d	
e	
f	
g	
h	

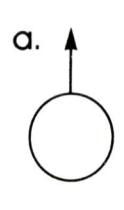

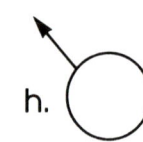

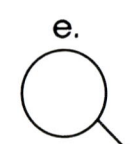

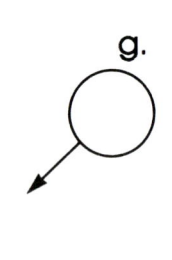

How well did I do?

Skates

Test roller skates or roller boots on different floor surfaces.

You need: roller boots or skates, tape measure.

Investigate.

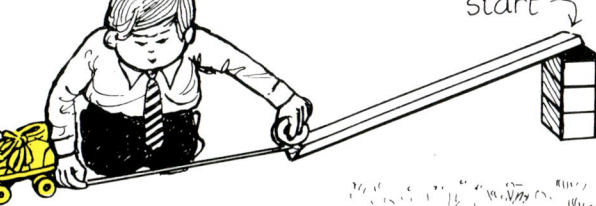

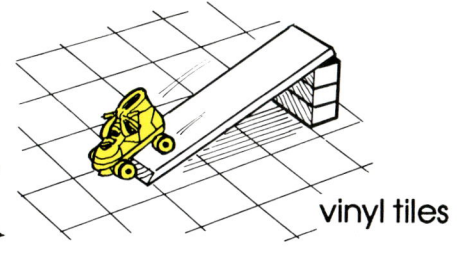

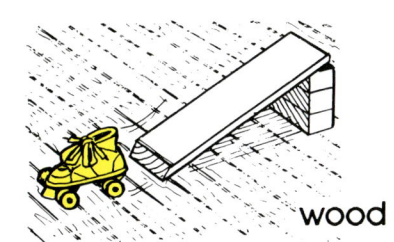

- Roll each skate down a ramp.
- Keep the height the same.

vinyl tiles

wood

grass

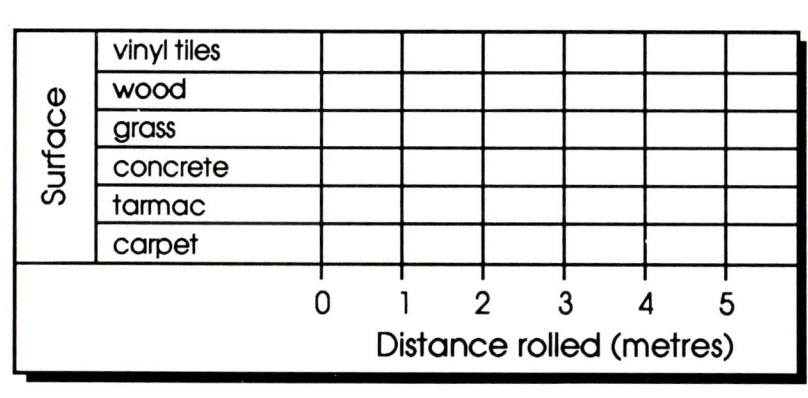

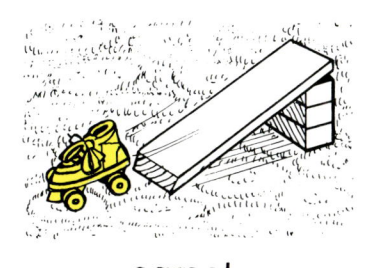

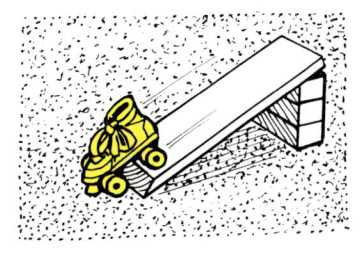

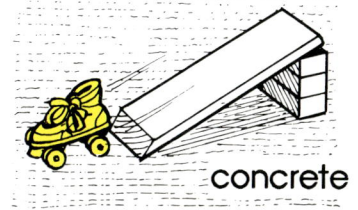

Surface						
vinyl tiles						
wood						
grass						
concrete						
tarmac						
carpet						

Distance rolled (metres) 0 1 2 3 4 5

Which floor surface is best for skating? See if you can explain why.

carpet

tarmac

concrete

- The best surface for skating is _____ because _____

How well did I do?

© Folens.

Drop it!

You need: 2 pieces of newspaper of the same size.

Investigate.

- Roll one piece of paper into a ball. Hold the ball in one hand.
- Hold the other flat paper in your other hand and drop them together.

1. Did they land together? _____
   _____

2. What happened to the ball? _____
   _____

3. What happened to the flat paper? _____
   _____

Record.

- Try this with some other objects of different shapes but made out of the same materials.
- Write down at least two more things that fall slowly to Earth.

_____
_____
_____

- Talk about why you think this happens.

USEFUL WORDS

slowly

quickly

floated

How well did I do?

20   © Folens.

In a spin

You need: a strip of paper about 15-20cm long and 3-5cm wide.

Investigate.

- Tear about one third of the way down the strip and fold in the sides.
- Hold it as high above the floor as you can and then let it go.
- Watch the strip carefully as it falls.

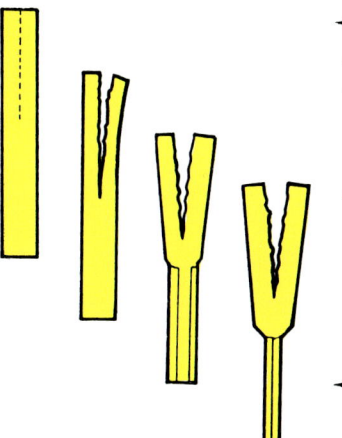

1. Did the strip spin? _____

2. Which way did it spin? _____

Record.

- Try to make it spin the opposite way.

- Change the design of your shape so that it falls more slowly. It must keep spinning until it reaches the floor!
- Draw your new design in this space:

How well did I do?

Pretty Polly

- Make a balancing parrot.

You need:

glue

scissors

card

brass fasteners

mini and maxi straws

template of parrot (page 23)

The perch

1. 2 slits about 1cm long

2. open out and glue

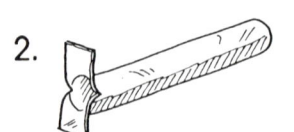

3. wrap flaps to join

The base

4. 4 slits

5. open into 'star'

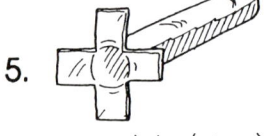

6. glue down for pillars, posts, hinges etc.

7. Cut out a parrot shape.

fix a short maxi straw

8. Make a perch.

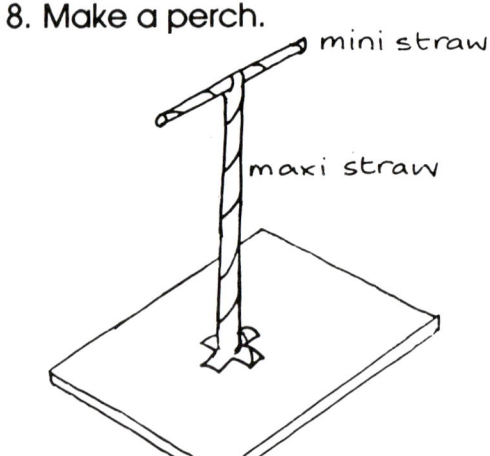

mini straw

maxi straw

9. Strengthen your perch if it needs it.

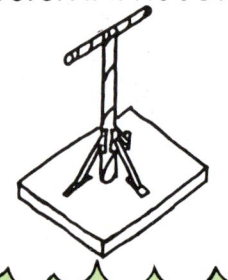

10. Slide the parrot on to the perch.

11. Add Blu-Tack to make it balance.

How well did I do?

© Folens.

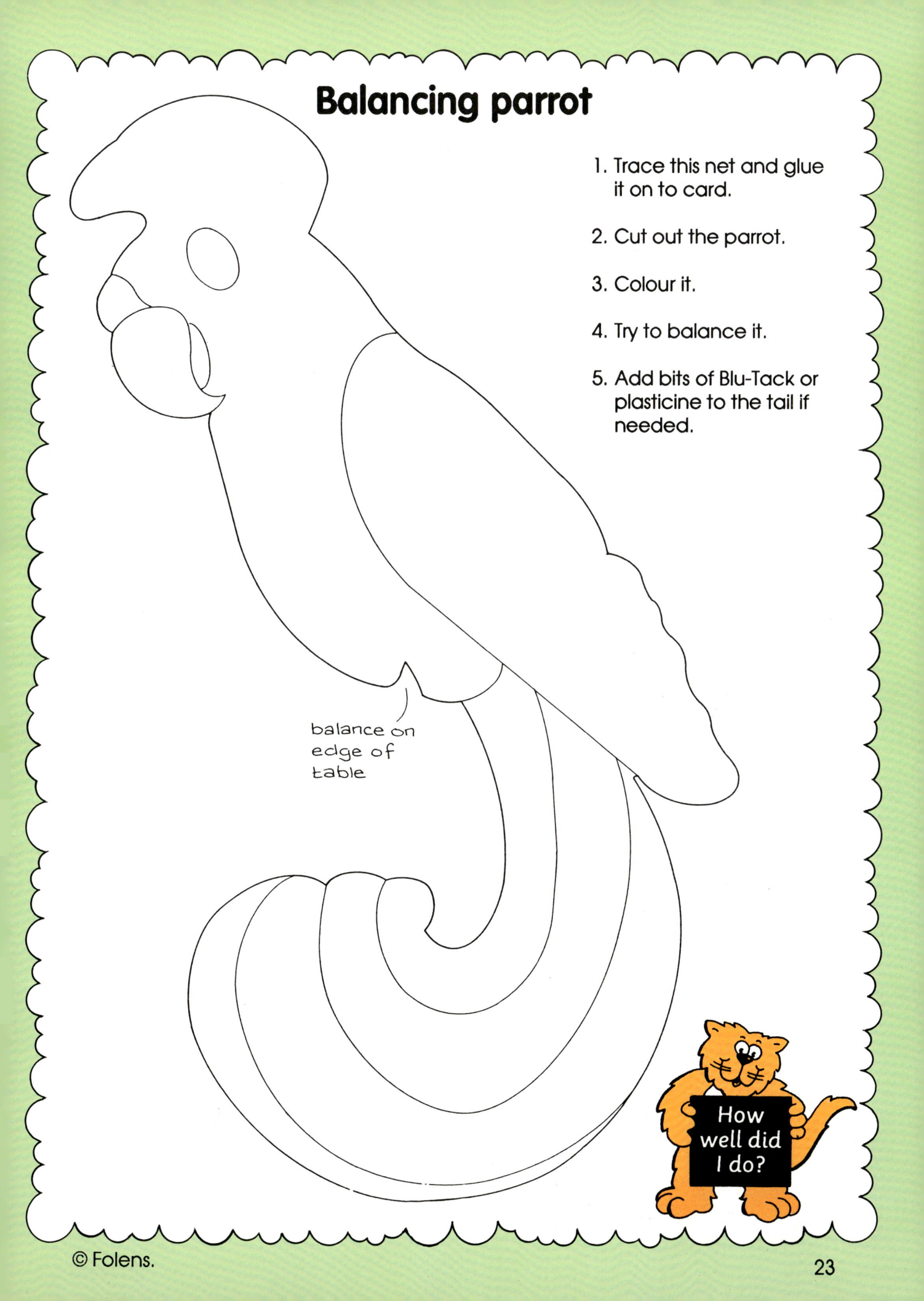

Balancing parrot

1. Trace this net and glue it on to card.

2. Cut out the parrot.

3. Colour it.

4. Try to balance it.

5. Add bits of Blu-Tack or plasticine to the tail if needed.

balance on edge of table

How well did I do?

© Folens.

It's pneumatic

You need: a balloon, balloon pump, heavy books.

Do not put balloons in your mouth.

"Investigate."

- Put the balloon on the edge of the table.
- Put the books on top of the balloon.
- Use the pump to blow air into the balloon.
- Watch what happens to the books.

1. What did you see happening to the books?

   _____

2. How many books could be lifted?

   _____

3. What lifted the books?

   _____

4. List some objects which use the strength of air to lift something?

   _____

   _____

- Does a foot pump on a car tyre lift the whole car?

   _____

"Record."

USEFUL WORDS

lifted

upwards

air

How well did I do?

Shadows

How can we make a shadow bigger?

You need: scissors, card, ruler, torch, plasticine.

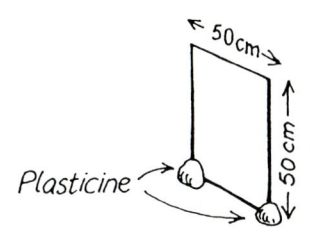

- Trace this figure, cut it out and glue it on to card.
- Stand it in front of a card screen.

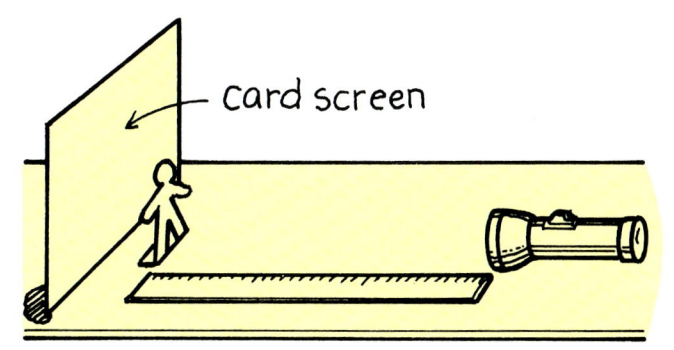

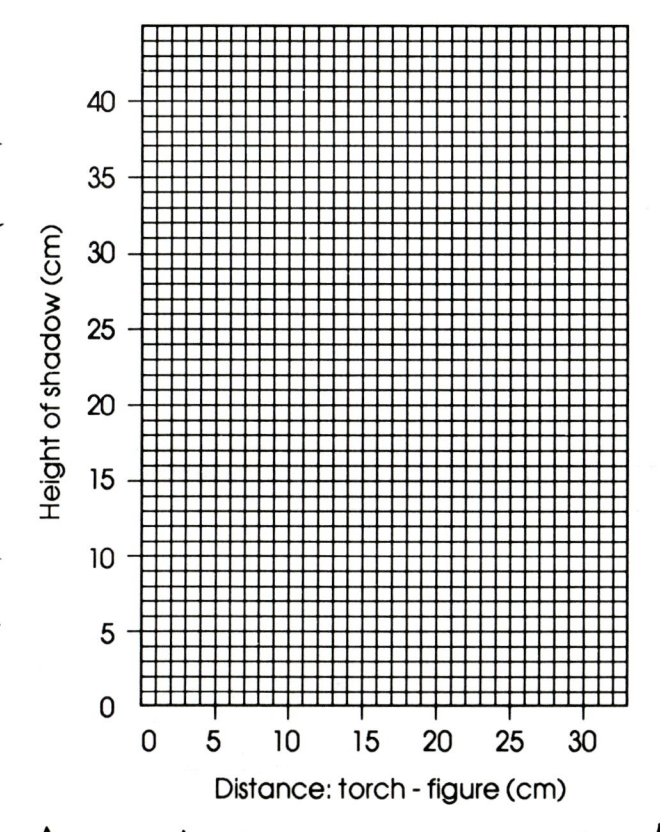

Cut the heavy lines

Score this line

- Measure the height of the shadow when the torch is at: 5cm, 10cm and 20cm from the figure.
  Move the torch only!
- Record your findings on this graph:
- Mark the height of each shadow with a cross.
- Draw a line to join the crosses.

Height of shadow (cm)

Distance: torch - figure (cm)

How well did I do?

© Folens.

25

High or low?

Take care when stretching elastic bands.

Can you make high and low notes?

You need: elastic bands of different lengths.

Stretch an elastic band between two chair legs.

Pluck the stretched elastic band. Listen carefully.

- Tape the band into the correct place below:

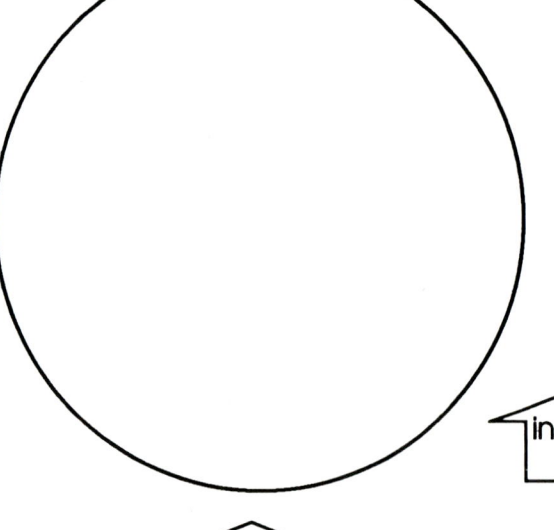

⬆ high notes   ⬆ in between notes   ⬆ low notes

- Test the other elastic bands and record in the same way.

- How can you tell whether an elastic band will make a high or low note?

_____

How well did I do?

26

© Folens.

What a noise!

Some children tested their toys.

They asked a friend to play each toy from behind a closed door.

They found out which was the loudest toy.

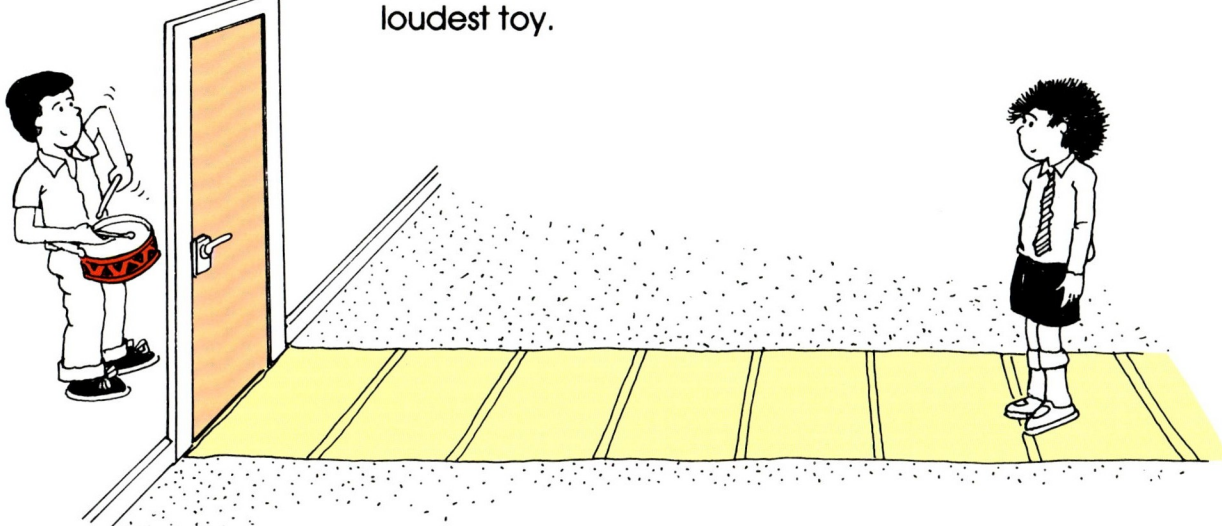

They measured.   They marked each metre.

They recorded their findings on a graph:

Toy											
drum											
trumpet											
whistle											
keyboard											
guitar											
harmonica											
	0	5	10	15	20	25	30	35	40	45	50

Distance heard (metres)

- Which toy can be heard furthest away?

_____

- Which is the loudest?

_____

How well did I do?

Is it attracted?

Investigate.

- Touch each object with the magnet.

magnet
pencil
plastic ruler
paper clip
piece of copper wire
drawing pin
pebble
safety pin
pair of scissors
nail
knife
apple
cotton reel

Record.

1. Which objects did the magnet attract or pick up?

a. _____   d. _____

b. _____   e. _____

c. _____   f. _____

2. Draw a circle around the things which are attracted by magnets.

    stone   wood   metal   plastic

3. Do magnets attract things made of stone, wood,

    metal or plastic? _____

4. Are all metals attracted by magnets? _____

- Try touching the magnet with other objects.
- List those which are attracted.

_____

_____

How well did I do?

Folens Flying Start
Starting Key Stage 2 Science

Guidance for parents and carers

The children's pages provide activities which will help to develop children's knowledge, understanding and skills across a wide range of science: the living world, the material world and the physical world. They have been carefully selected to cover a large range of ability levels. Your child may find some of them very easy and some too difficult. Noticing his/her achievement will help you to decide which books will provide the support which s/he needs.

Workbooks are intended for children to write or draw in. Many of the activities in this *Starting Science* book require only the use of a pencil, but the value of practical activities which involve children in handling and observing things around them, should not be underestimated. Some activities therefore involve the use of materials which can be found in most homes.

Working together

Reading together

- Whenever possible, work **with** your child. In some activities this is essential.
- In some cases children may need help in reading instructions.
- Choose a time when the child (and you!) are relaxed, and not already engaged in any other activity.
- Work in a comfortable place.
- Attempt only one or two activities, unless the child wishes to continue. Children learn best when they are interested! Remember that the time for which chidren can concentrate varies. As a rule the younger the child, the shorter his/her concentration, but even the youngest children may surprise you if something really captures their interest. Watch for signs of restlessness, and stop!
- Read the notes on these pages, and the children's pages, in preparation, before the child begins.
- Try, whenever appropriate, to relate the activities in the book to everyday life, sometimes before the child has attempted the activity, sometimes afterwards, but do not make the mistake of turning every occasion into a lesson! Some ideas are suggested.
- Do not worry about any gaps in your own science background. The best teachers are always prepared to admit that they do not know, but will find out, or often work it out with the child. Answers and guidance are provided, but space does not permit detailed discussion. Reference books are always useful. It will be noticed that often there is not a 'right answer', or the answer depends on a number of possibilities. Discussion helps the learner to sort out his/her ideas.
- Praise the child for his/her achievement. Avoid becoming irritable/sounding disappointed if s/he finds an activity too difficult. You could say something like, "You'll be able to do that when you've had more practice." On completion of each page ask the child to choose a sticker to show how well s/he has done, and to stick it in the box provided.

Living World
Animal round up - *(page 2)*
This requires careful observation, while drawing on the child's knowledge of animal characteristics. It develops understanding of classification of animals. *Answers*:

What can you see?	Which animals look like that?	Animal group name
scaly dry skin	lizard, snake	reptiles
scaly wet skin	goldfish, eel	fish
smooth skin	newt, frog	amphibians
feathery skin	blue-tit, seagull	birds
hairy skin	cat, mouse	mammals

Birds, reptiles, amphibians and fish lay eggs. Mammals do not. Mammals give birth to live young which they suckle. Another group, not featured here is insects, including flies, butterflies, moths, bees, wasps, and other creatures which have 6 legs and a body in three parts. Spiders are not insects, as they have 8 legs, neither are millipedes, centipedes, worms, snails nor slugs. A term which can be used for these other small creatures whose group is not known is 'minibeasts', which is not a scientific word, but very useful. The child could look for other examples of these groups of animals. More work on animal grouping appears in *Key Stage 2 Living World Science* and was introduced in *Key Stage 1 Living World Science*.

Air, land and water - *(page 3)*
This helps to develop understanding of the variety of animal life and how to classify animals. Here the animals are classified according to where they are found. Some animals may be found in more than one place. The child should write the name of the

© Folens.

animal, using the key to identify it, in the correct set. The part where sets overlap is for animals which are found in either land or water.
A correct answer should look like this:

Venn diagram with "land" and "water" circles:
- land only: kingfisher
- overlap: mute swan, mallard, Canada goose, great crested grebe, heron
- water only: tadpole, pike, salmon

Food chains - *(page 4)*
The interdependence of living things is introduced here. The convention for showing food chains is with arrows pointing from plants towards animals.
Answers:
grass -> sheep -> person
wheat -> harvest mouse -> barn owl
pond weed -> goldfish -> cat

In the pet shop, questions such as, "What does it eat?" and "What eats it?" help to develop understanding of food chains. Talk about what familiar animals eat, and what eats them.

Ways to move - *(page 5)*
This looks at the different ways in which animals move. The child will develop understanding of similarities and differences between animals. Some move in more than one way. The sorting sets: 'fly', 'creep' and 'hop' overlap. Animals which move in more than one way should be placed in the overlapping parts:

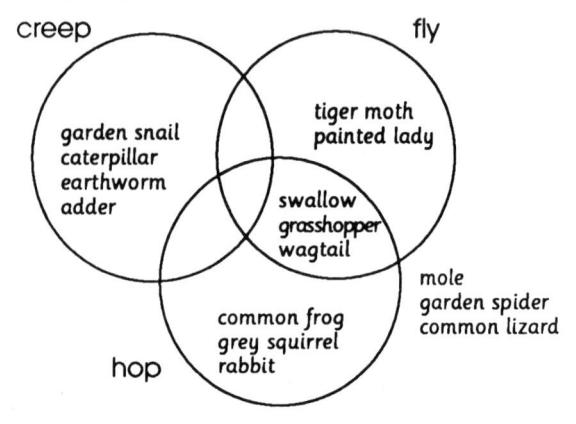

Three overlapping circles: creep, fly, hop
- creep only: garden snail, caterpillar, earthworm, adder
- fly only: tiger moth, painted lady
- creep/fly/hop overlap: swallow, grasshopper, wagtail
- creep/hop overlap: common frog, grey squirrel, rabbit
- outside: mole, garden spider, common lizard

Some animals do not fit in any of these sets. They are listed outside them.

Smudge bugs - *(page 6)*
Skills of observation and measurement are developed here. The child completes a graph, then uses the data to answer questions. The bugs should be measured across the longest/widest part of the body. The legs do not count. The child should write the size of each bug on its body, as a record of which have been measured.

The completed graph should look like this:

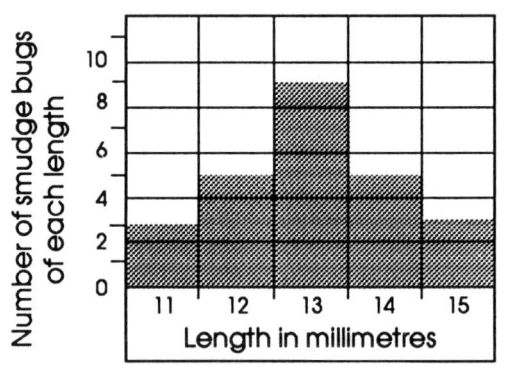

Bar graph — Number of smudge bugs of each length vs Length in millimetres (11–15); bar at 13 reaches highest (~9).

Answers:
1. 3 2. 3 3. 13mm

A simpler sorting/classifying activity appears in *Starting Key Stage 1 Science*. See also *Key Stage 2 Living World Science*.

Sight tests - *(page 7)*
This is not a competition to show whose eyesight is the best, but an investigation to find out about the differences/similarities between people. Notice the discussion points which will help the child to interpret his/her findings.

Finger press ups - *(page 8)*
To make this a fair test the child should ensure that everyone tested carries out the finger press ups in the same way. A rule, such as 'The ends of the peg must meet during each finger press up,' could help. Encourage the child to look for patterns in his/her findings: e.g. Does the same person seem to be the quickest at right and left hand press ups? What does the child think makes some people better at these? (bigger hands? stronger fingers? practice in activities where the fingers are used, e.g. playing the piano?)

Jump! - *(page 9)*
Here is a close look at how we move. It is much easier to jump in some directions than others. This practical investigation should reveal all! For jumping up the child should first mark the highest point which can be reached, stretching with the feet flat, then jump and measure the difference between the two marks. Otherwise the person's height plus the jump is being measured, not just the jump. Ask the child what s/he can do to jump further. Do some of the jumps yourself, for him/her to observe! Increased distance/height are gained by bending the knees first, and swinging the arms in the direction of the jump.

Our changing world - *(page 10)*
Environmental awareness can be developed by discussion, also by example. Do you recycle glass, paper, plastic, metal? Do you avoid waste of these resources, and fuels? How much water do you waste? Do you waste fuel?

© Folens.

The Material World

How do they compare? - (page 11)

Awareness of the differences and similarities between common materials is a starting point for understanding why materials are used for particular purposes. Useful classifications are: 'solid', 'liquid' and 'gas'. Ask: "Does it melt at room temperature?", "Is it hard?" "Can you bend it?" "Can you twist it?" "If you put it in different containers does its shape change or stay the same?"

Answers:

Materials	How are they alike?	How are they different?
rubber paper	Can be bent and twisted. Can be squashed.	Paper cannot be stretched. Rubber can be stretched. Rubber bounces higher.
paper aluminium (kitchen foil)	Can be folded and twisted. Can be screwed into a ball. Can be cut with scissors.	Aluminium foil does not burn. Paper burns. You can see your reflection in foil but not in paper.
aluminium ice	Both are solid.	Ice melts in a room. Aluminium does not.
ice water	Both can be eaten. They are both made of water.	Ice is solid. Water is liquid. Water can travel through a tube. Ice cannot.
water air	Both can travel through tubes.	Air is a gas. Water is a liquid.

House on fire - (page 12)

Safety aspects of materials is a vital learning point. Dangers here are: oil heater placed where it can be knocked over, electric blanket left on for too long, old electric heater, smoking in bed (or anywhere!), neglected naked flame (candle), pan handles where they can be knocked over, neglected iron, cigarette ends left burning, dangerously stacked materials in fireplace, no fireguard. Ask the child how fire accidents can be prevented. Look for 'flame resistant' labels on garments. Does your home have a fire drill? Most do not, but it could save lives. Ask the child to think of a fire drill. Contact your local fire station for information.

Dissolving - (page 13)

Hygiene is important here. The child should not return used foods to the kitchen, since soil and sand are also tested. Use disposable containers. Provide an old spoon. Children often describe things which dissolve as 'melting' which is not the same. Melting is changing from solid to liquid, e.g. ice lolly, butter, chocolate, when warm. If no particles of the material can be seen in the water it has dissolved. Each one may be stirred. Sugar and salt are soluble, but sand and soil are not. To find out whether they dissolve **more easily** in hot water, the child could time how long the salt, and the sugar take to dissolve in cold, then in warm water. To make it a 'fair test' each should be stirred equally.

It's not fair! - (pages 14-15)

An important scientific skill is 'fair testing'. A fair test here means that all possibilities are considered, and that 'variables are controlled'. Jagtar assumes that it is the washing up liquid which makes the water spread out (as it happens, correctly), but there are 2 possible variables which could have caused the water to spread:
1. putting wax on the paper
2. dipping a pin in washing up liquid then touching the drop of water with it.

The child is asked to suggest a fair way to carry out this investigation. This would mean placing a drop of water on plain paper then waxed paper, and testing each with a pin coated in washing up liquid, also with a clean pin. The child should try to think of a fair test before looking at page 15, which gives clues. The chart helps children who find it difficult to plan fair tests without help. See also *Key Stage 2 Material World Science*.

Reading a thermometer - (page 16)

Recording the weather requires understanding of thermometers. If possible provide a thermometer of the type shown. Children in British schools usually measure in the Celsius (centigrade) scale. Celsius is the name of the person who devised it. Avoid mercury-filled thermometers, which are dangerous if dropped, as mercury is poisonous. (Mercury is grey; alcohol filled thermometers contain a red or blue liquid.) Most of the page may be completed without using a real thermometer. This is required for the last question only. With practice children should be able to estimate the air temperature each day. They could use a thermometer to check their estimates.

Weatherwise - (page 17)

This develops understanding of signs and symbols and skills of observation.

Answers:

	Weather symbol meanings
7	rain
2	bright sunshine: temperature 25oC
6	snow
9	thunderstorm
4	rain with sunny intervals
8	sleet
3	thick dull cloud
5	fine but cloudy
1	cloudy with sunny intervals

Look at television, newspapers, weather forecasts and weather maps.

Blowing in the wind - (page 18)

Prepare for this by looking for weather vanes and windsocks. Weather vanes spin around and face the direction from which the wind is coming. Windsocks blow away from the wind direction. The child may need some practice with compass directions. See also *Key Stage 1* and *Key Stage 2 Material World Science*.

© Folens.

Answers:

Symbol	Type of wind
a	southerly
b	south westerly
c	easterly
d	westerly
e	north westerly
f	northerly
g	north easterly
h	south easterly

The Physical World

Skates - *(page 19)*
This draws attention to what stops things moving. It is not that they run out of energy. Energy is needed to provide a force to make a skate or other object move. Once moving it keeps going until something stops it. The skate gets its energy to start moving by being raised on a plank. Air resistance and friction are the forces which usually slow things down and eventually stop them, unless they have an energy supply to keep them going. The skate will probably roll furthest on vinyl tiles. Fair testing is important. The child should ensure that the ramp is always at the same height. The height of the ramp is a **variable** which must be kept the same. The variable which is changed is the floor surface.

Drop it! - *(page 20)*
Like the previous activity, this develops understanding of the forces involved in movement. Gravity is the force which starts the pieces of paper moving. A flat piece of paper covers a greater area, and so more air resistance means that it is slowed down. It is not **weight**, but **shape** which is the important factor in how quickly things fall.

In a spin - *(page 21)*
A piece of paper torn as shown with the 2 fins bent in opposite directions should spin as it falls. The shape of the paper affects the way it falls. Air catches the fins and pushes against them. The direction of spin may be changed by changing the directions in which the fins are bent. Sycamore seeds spin in a similar way.

Pretty Polly and **Balancing Parrot** - *(pages 22-23)*
This practical activity requires a few simple materials, including straws of different widths. Plastic straws are difficult to glue. Use the paper ones sold in modelling shops. Practical skills will be developed: working with tools and materials, while the child learns about the forces involved in balance.

It's pneumatic - *(page 24)*
Pneumatic means using air. A balloon can store energy as compressed air. Air is forced into the balloon, and so is under pressure. Compressed air can exert a strong force. Here it can be used to lift books. Help the child to develop understanding of the power of air by looking for uses of it locally: pumps used to lift things, air brakes (the air can usually be heard escaping).

Shadows - *(page 25)*
Remind the child that only one **variable** is to be changed: the torch (a powerful torch is best). You could use a wall instead of the card screen. The figure and the screen must stay in the same place. The child should find that the nearer the torch is to the figure, the larger the shadow. This is because a shadow is an absence of light. More light is blocked out if the figure is near the torch. The child may be able to think of other ways to change the size of the shadow: moving either the figure or the screen. Can s/he make a shadow which is smaller than the figure? S/he can do this by holding the torch directly above the figure. Use this to help develop the understanding of shadows made by the sun. Shadows are shortest when it is overhead, and longest when it is lower in the sky. The graph should be marked with crosses. The actual results may differ slightly.

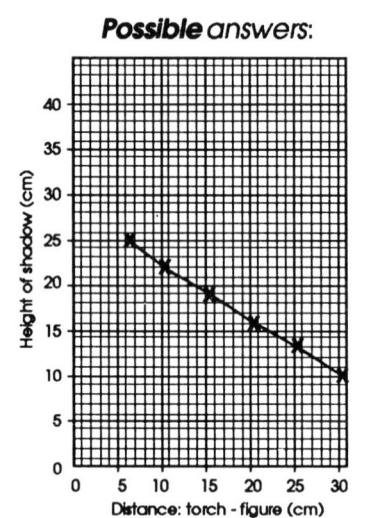

Possible *answers*:

High or low? - *(page 26)*
Children often find it difficult to distinguish between high and low sounds. 'High' should not be confused with 'loud', or 'low' with 'quiet'. Short elastic bands make higher sounds than long ones, because small things vibrate more quickly than large ones.

What a noise! - *(page 27)*
The child is asked to interpret data presented as a graph. The toy which was heard furthest away was the whistle. The whistle is therefore the loudest.

Is it attracted? - *(page 28)*
You need a magnet and a collection of everyday objects. First ask the child to predict what will be attracted to the magnet. S/he may think that **all** metals are attracted - only iron and steel are. (Steel is made from iron.) Some 'tin' cans are attracted because they are made from steel, coated with a layer of tin. The magnet attracts the steel through the tin. Aluminium cans for recycling, are sorted from steel ones using a magnet, since aluminium is not attracted. Cobalt and nickel are also magnetic, but these are not so likely to be found around the home. A strong magnet will attract some audio tapes. Do not try it on your favourites!

© Folens.